Machine Learning

Intermediate's Guide with R/Python

Thomas Farth

Copyright © 2018 by Thomas Farth
All Rights Reserved.

Contents

Chapter 1: Recap of Beginner's Guide to Machine Learning 5
   1.1   Machine Learning & its Applications 6
   1.2   Machine Learning in Practice 7
   1.3   Mathematical Foundation for Machine Learning and AI 8
   1.4   Programming Languages 9
   1.5   Introduction to MLib (Apache Spark) 10

Chapter 2: Python for Machine Learning 12
   2.1 Getting Started 13
      2.1.1 Environment Setup 13
      2.1.2 Writing First Program 14
   2.2 Variables & Assigning Values 14
   2.3 Basic Operators 17
   2.6 Decision Making 20
   2.7 Loop 21
   2.8 Modules 26

Chapter 3: R for Machine Learning 29
   3.1 Getting Started 30
      3.1.1 Environmental Setup 31
   3.2 Data Types 33
   3.3 Variables 36
   3.4 Operators 37
   3.5 Decision Making 43
   3.6 Loops 44
   3.7 Functions 46

Chapter 4: Types of Machine Learning 49
   4.1 Types of Machine Learning 51
      4.1.1 Supervised Machine Learning 51
      4.1.2 Unsupervised Machine Learning 52
      4.1.3 Reinforcement Machine Learning 53
   4.2 Data Processing 53
      4.2.1 Techniques for Data Preprocessing 55

Chapter 5: Regression & Classification 59
   5.1 Regression 60
      5.1.1 Regression Analysis 60
      5.1.2 Terminologies 61
      5.1.3 Types of Regression 62
   5.2 Classification 66
      5.2.1 Terminologies 66
      5.2.2 Types of Classification 68

Chapter 6: Clustering 72
   6.1 Introduction 74
   6.2 Types of Clustering Methods 75
      6.2.1 Distribution Based Method 75
      6.2.2 Centroid Based Method 75
      6.2.3 Connectivity Based Methods 76
      6.2.4 Density Models 76
   6.3 Clustering Algorithms 76
      6.3.1 K-Means Clustering 77
   6.4 Applications 77

Chapter 7: Natural Language Processing, Reinforcement Learning 79
   7.1 Natural Language Processing 80
      7.1.1 Introduction 81
      7.1.2 Components of NLP 82
      7.1.3 NLP Terminology 83
   7.2 Reinforcement Learning 84
      7.2.1 Building Blocks: Environment and Agent 85

Chapter 8: Conclusion 87
   8.1 Conclusion 88

Chapter 1

Recap of Beginner's Guide to Machine Learning

1.1 Machine Learning & its Applications

As we discussed in **Beginner's Guide to Machine Learning** machine learning involves building mathematical models to help understand data. "Learning" enters the fray when we give these models tunable parameters that can be adapted to observed data; in this way the program can be considered to be "learning" from the data. Once these models have been fit to previously seen data, they can be used to predict and understand aspects of newly observed data. I'll leave to the reader the more philosophical digression regarding the extent to which this type of mathematical, model-based "learning" is similar to the "learning" exhibited by the human brain.

Machine learning is an application of artificial intelligence (AI) that provides systems the ability to automatically learn and improve from experience without being explicitly programmed. Machine learning focuses on the development of computer programs that can access data and use it learn for themselves.

The process of learning begins with observations or data, such as examples, direct experience, or instruction, in order to look for patterns in data and make better decisions in the future based on the examples that we provide. The primary aim is to allow the computers learn automatically without human intervention or assistance and adjust actions accordingly.

1.2 Machine Learning in Practice

Machine learning algorithms are only a very small part of using machine learning in practice as a data analyst or data scientist. In practice, the process often looks like:

- **Start Loop**
✓ Understand the domain, prior knowledge and goals. Talk to domain experts. Often the goals are very unclear. You often have more things to try then you can possibly implement.
✓ Data integration, selection, cleaning and pre-processing. This is often the most time-consuming part. It is important to have high quality data. The more data you have, the more it sucks because the data is dirty. Garbage in, garbage out.
✓ Learning models. The fun part. This part is very mature. The tools are general.
✓ Interpreting results. Sometimes it does not matter how the model works as long it delivers results. Other domains require that the model is understandable. You will be challenged by human experts.
✓ Consolidating and deploying discovered knowledge. The majority of projects that are successful in the lab are not used in practice. It is very hard to get something used.
- **End Loop**

It is not a one-shot process, it is a cycle. You need to run the loop until you get a result that you can use in practice. Also, the data can change, requiring a new loop.

1.3 Mathematical Foundation for Machine Learning and AI

In this section, we discussed about the mathematical objects of Linear Algebra that are used in Machine Learning. You learned how to multiply, divide, add and subtract these mathematical objects. Furthermore, you have learned about the most important properties of Matrices and why they enable us to make more efficient computations. On top of that, you have learned what inverse and transpose Matrices are and what you can do with them. Although there are also other parts of Linear Algebra used in Machine Learning, this section gave you a proper introduction to the most important concepts.

Machine learning uses derivatives in optimization problems. Optimization algorithms like gradient descent use derivatives to decide whether to increase or decrease weights in order to maximize or minimize some objective (e.g. a model's accuracy or error functions). Derivatives also help us approximate nonlinear functions as linear functions (tangent lines), which have constant slopes. With a constant slope we can decide whether to move up or down the slope (increase or decrease our weights) to get closer to the target value (class label).

Machine Learning and Statistics aren't very different fields. Actually, someone recently defined Machine Learning as 'doing statistics on a Mac'. Some of the fundamental Statistical and Probability Theory needed for ML are Combinatorics, Probability Rules & Axioms, Bayes' Theorem, Random Variables, Variance and Expectation,

Conditional and Joint Distributions, Standard Distributions (Bernoulli, Binomial, Multinomial, Uniform and Gaussian), Moment Generating Functions, Maximum Likelihood Estimation (MLE), Prior and Posterior, Maximum a Posteriori Estimation (MAP) and Sampling Methods.

The difficult part is that we all live in a chaotic universe where things can't be measured exactly most of the time. When we study real world processes we want to learn about numerous random events that distort our experiments. Uncertainty is everywhere and we must take it to be used for our needs. That is when probability theory and statistics come into play.

Nowadays those disciplines lie in the center of artificial intelligence, particle physics, social science, bio-informatics and in our everyday lives.

1.4 Programming Languages

As we know high-level languages are designed to be easy to read and understand. This allows programmers to write source code in a natural fashion, using logical words and symbols. For example, reserved words like function, while, if, and else are used in most major programming languages. Symbols like <, >, ==, and != are common operators. Many high-level languages are similar enough that programmers can easily understand source code written in multiple languages.

We discussed earlier there's so much more activity in machine learning than job offers in the West can describe, however, and peer opinions are of course very valuable but often conflicting and as such may confuse the novices. We turned instead to our hard data from 2,000+ data scientists and machine learning developers who responded to our latest survey about which languages they use and what projects they're working on — along with many other interesting things about their machine learning activities and training. Then, being data scientists ourselves, we couldn't help but run a few models to see which are the most important factors that are correlated to language selection.

Python is considered to be in the first place in the list of all AI development languages due to the simplicity. The syntaxes belonging to python are very simple and can be easily learnt. Therefore, many AI algorithms can be easily implemented in it. Python takes short development time in comparison to other languages like Java, C++ or Ruby. Python supports object oriented, functional as well as procedure-oriented styles of programming.

1.5 Introduction to MLib (Apache Spark)

As we discussed Spark provides a machine learning library known as MLlib. Spark MLlib provides various machine learning algorithms such as classification, regression, clustering, and collaborative filtering. It also provides tools such as featurization, pipelines, persistence, and utilities for handling linear algebra operations, statistics and data handling.

The popular algorithms and utilities in Spark MLlib are:

- Basic Statistics
- Regression
- Classification
- Recommendation System
- Clustering
- Dimensionality Reduction
- Feature Extraction
- Optimization

Now we will discuss machine learning algorithms in depth in next chapters.

Chapter 2

Python for Machine Learning

2.1 Getting Started

Python is a widely used high-level programming language for general-purpose programming, created by Guido van Rossum and first released in 1991. Python features a dynamic type system and automatic memory management and supports multiple programming paradigms, including object-oriented, imperative, functional programming, and procedural styles. It has a large and comprehensive standard library.

Two major versions of Python are currently in active use:

- Python 3.x is the current version and is under active development.
- Python 2.x is the legacy version and will receive only security updates until 2020. No new features will be implemented. Note that many projects still use Python 2, although migrating to Python 3 is getting easier.

2.1.1 Environment Setup

Before we start Python programming, we need to have an interpreter to interpret and run our programs.

Windows: There are many interpreters available freely to run Python scripts like IDLE (Integrated Development Environment) which is installed when you install the python software from http://python.org/

Linux: For Linux, Python comes bundled with the Linux.

2.1.2 Writing First Program
Following is first program in Python

```
# Script Begins

print("Hello World")

# Scripts Ends
```

Output: Hello World

2.2 Variables & Assigning Values

Variables are nothing but reserved memory locations to store values. This means that when you create a variable you reserve some space in memory.

Based on the data type of a variable, the interpreter allocates memory and decides what can be stored in the reserved memory. Therefore, by assigning different data types to variables, you can store integers, decimals or characters in these variables.

Python variables do not need explicit declaration to reserve memory space. The declaration happens automatically when you assign a value to a variable. The equal sign (=) is used to assign values to variables.

The operand to the left of the = operator is the name of the variable and the operand to the right of the =

operator is the value stored in the variable. For example –

```
counter = 100        # An integer assignment

miles   = 1000.0     # A floating point

name    = "John"     # A string
```

Python has five standard data types –

- Numbers
- String
- List
- Tuple
- Dictionary

Strings in Python are identified as a contiguous set of characters represented in the quotation marks. Python allows for either pairs of single or double quotes. Subsets of strings can be taken using the slice operator ([ ] and [:]) with indexes starting at 0 in the beginning of the string and working their way from -1 at the end.

```
list = [ 'abcd', 786 , 2.23, 'john', 70.2 ]

tinylist = [123, 'john']
```

A tuple is another sequence data type that is similar to the list. A tuple consists of a number of values separated by commas. Unlike lists, however, tuples are enclosed within parentheses.

The main differences between lists and tuples are: Lists are enclosed in brackets ([ ]) and their elements and size can be changed, while tuples are enclosed in parentheses (( )) and cannot be updated. Tuples can be thought of as **read-only** lists. For example –

```
tuple = ( 'abcd', 786 , 2.23, 'john', 70.2  )

tinytuple = (123, 'john')
```

Python's dictionaries are kind of hash table type. They work like associative arrays or hashes found in Perl and consist of key-value pairs. A dictionary key can be almost any Python type, but are usually numbers or strings. Values, on the other hand, can be any arbitrary Python object.

Dictionaries are enclosed by curly braces ({ }) and values can be assigned and accessed using square braces ([]). For example

```
dict = {}

dict['one'] = "This is one"

dict[2]    = "This is two"

tinydict = {'name': 'john','code':6734, 'dept': 'sales'}
```

2.3 Basic Operators

Operators are the constructs which can manipulate the value of operands.

Consider the expression 4 + 5 = 9. Here, 4 and 5 are called operands and + is called operator.

Types of Operator

Python language supports the following types of operators.

- Arithmetic Operators
- Comparison (Relational) Operators
- Assignment Operators
- Logical Operators
- Bitwise Operators
- Membership Operators
- Identity Operators

Arithmetic Operators:

Operator	Description	Example
+ Addition	Adds values on either side of the operator.	a + b = 30
- Subtraction	Subtracts right hand operand from left hand operand.	a – b = -10
* Multiplication	Multiplies values on either side of the operator	a * b = 200
/ Division	Divides left hand operand by right hand operand	b / a = 2

% Modulus	Divides left hand operand by right hand operand and returns remainder	b % a = 0
** Exponent	Performs exponential (power) calculation on operators	a**b =10 to the power 20

Comparison Operators:

Operator	Description	Example
==	If the values of two operands are equal, then the condition becomes true.	(a == b) is not true.
!=	If values of two operands are not equal, then condition becomes true.	(a != b) is true.
<>	If values of two operands are not equal, then condition becomes true.	(a <> b) is true. This is similar to != operator.
>	If the value of left operand is greater than the value of right operand, then condition becomes true.	(a > b) is not true.
<	If the value of left operand is less than the value of right operand, then condition becomes true.	(a < b) is true.
>=	If the value of left operand is	(a >= b) is

	greater than or equal to the value of right operand, then condition becomes true.	not true.
<=	If the value of left operand is less than or equal to the value of right operand, then condition becomes true.	(a <= b) is true.

Assignment Operators:

Operator	Description	Example
=	Assigns values from right side operands to left side operand	c = a + b assigns value of a + b into c
+= Add AND	It adds right operand to the left operand and assign the result to left operand	c += a is equivalent to c = c + a
-= Subtract AND	It subtracts right operand from the left operand and assign the result to left operand	c -= a is equivalent to c = c - a
*= Multiply AND	It multiplies right operand with the left operand and assign the result to left operand	c *= a is equivalent to c = c * a
/= Divide AND	It divides left operand with the right operand and assign the result to	c /= a is equivalent to c = c / ac /= a is equivalent to c = c

	left operand	/ a
%= Modulus AND	It takes modulus using two operands and assign the result to left operand	c %= a is equivalent to c = c % a
**= Exponent AND	Performs exponential (power) calculation on operators and assign value to the left operand	c **= a is equivalent to c = c ** a
//= Floor Division	It performs floor division on operators and assign value to the left operand	c //= a is equivalent to c = c // a

2.6 Decision Making

Decision making is anticipation of conditions occurring while execution of the program and specifying actions taken according to the conditions.

Decision structures evaluate multiple expressions which produce TRUE or FALSE as outcome. You need to determine which action to take and which statements to execute if outcome is TRUE or FALSE otherwise.

Python programming language assumes any non-zero and non-null values as TRUE, and if it is either zero or null, then it is assumed as FALSE value.

Python programming language provides following types of decision-making statements.

```
var = 100

if ( var == 100 ) : print "Value of expression
is 100"

print "Good bye!"
```

2.7 Loop

In general, statements are executed sequentially: The first statement in a function is executed first, followed by the second, and so on. There may be a situation when you need to execute a block of code several number of times.

Programming languages provide various control structures that allow for more complicated execution paths.

A loop statement allows us to execute a statement or group of statements multiple times.

while loop:

A **while** loop statement in Python programming language repeatedly executes a target statement as long as a given condition is true. When the condition becomes false, program control passes to the line immediately following the loop.

In Python, all the statements indented by the same number of character spaces after a programming construct are considered to be part of a single block of code. Python uses indentation as its method of grouping statements.

```
count = 0

while (count < 9):

   print 'The count is:', count

   count = count + 1


print "Good bye!"
```

When the above code is executed, it produces the following result –

```
The count is: 0
The count is: 1
The count is: 2
The count is: 3
The count is: 4
The count is: 5
The count is: 6
The count is: 7
The count is: 8
Good bye!
```

for loop:

It has the ability to iterate over the items of any sequence, such as a list or a string. If a sequence contains an expression list, it is evaluated first. Then, the first item in the sequence is assigned to the iterating variable *iterating_var*. Next, the statements block is executed. Each item in the list is assigned to *iterating_var*, and the statement(s) block is executed until the entire sequence is exhausted.

```
for letter in 'Python':     # First Example
   print 'Current Letter :', letter


fruits = ['banana', 'apple', 'mango']
for fruit in fruits:        # Second Example
   print 'Current fruit :', fruit


print "Good bye!"
```

When the above code is executed, it produces the following result –

```
Current Letter : P
Current Letter : y
Current Letter : t
Current Letter : h
Current Letter : o
Current Letter : n
Current fruit : banana
Current fruit : apple
Current fruit : mango
Good bye!
```

Nested loops:

Python programming language allows to use one loop inside another loop. Following section shows few examples to illustrate the concept.

A final note on loop nesting is that you can put any type of loop inside of any other type of loop. For example a for loop can be inside a while loop or vice versa.

```
i = 2

while(i < 100):

  j = 2

  while(j <= (i/j)):

    if not(i%j): break
```

```
   j = j + 1

 if (j > i/j) : print i, " is prime"

 i = i + 1


print "Good bye!"
```

When the above code is executed, it produces following result –

```
2 is prime
3 is prime
5 is prime
7 is prime
11 is prime
13 is prime
17 is prime
19 is prime
23 is prime
29 is prime
31 is prime
37 is prime
41 is prime
43 is prime
47 is prime
53 is prime
59 is prime
61 is prime
```

67 is prime
71 is prime
73 is prime
79 is prime
83 is prime
89 is prime
97 is prime
Good bye!

2.8 Modules

A module allows you to logically organize your Python code. Grouping related code into a module makes the code easier to understand and use. A module is a Python object with arbitrarily named attributes that you can bind and reference.

Simply, a module is a file consisting of Python code. A module can define functions, classes and variables. A module can also include runnable code.

```
def print_func( par ):
   print "Hello : ", par
   return
```

Variables are names (identifiers) that map to objects. A *namespace* is a dictionary of variable names (keys) and their corresponding objects (values).

A Python statement can access variables in a *local namespace* and in the *global namespace*. If a local and a global variable have the same name, the local variable shadows the global variable.

Each function has its own local namespace. Class methods follow the same scoping rule as ordinary functions.

Python makes educated guesses on whether variables are local or global. It assumes that any variable assigned a value in a function is local.

Therefore, in order to assign a value to a global variable within a function, you must first use the global statement.

The statement *global VarName* tells Python that VarName is a global variable. Python stops searching the local namespace for the variable.

For example, we define a variable *Money* in the global namespace. Within the function *Money*, we assign *Money* a value, therefore Python assumes *Money* as a local variable. However, we accessed the value of the local variable *Money* before setting it, so an UnboundLocalError is the result. Uncommenting the global statement fixes the problem.

A package is a hierarchical file directory structure that defines a single Python application environment that consists of modules and subpackages and sub-subpackages, and so on.

Consider a file *Pots.py* available in *Phone* directory. This file has following line of source code –

```
#!/usr/bin/python

def Pots():

  print "I'm Pots Phone"
```

Similar way, we have another two files having different functions with the same name as above –

- *Phone/Isdn.py* file having function Isdn()
- *Phone/G3.py* file having function G3()

Now, create one more file __init__.py in *Phone* directory –

- Phone/__init__.py

To make all of your functions available when you've imported Phone, you need to put explicit import statements in __init__.py as follows –

```
from Pots import Pots
from Isdn import Isdn
from G3 import G3
```

After you add these lines to __init__.py, you have all of these classes available when you import the Phone package.

Chapter 3

R for Machine Learning

3.1 Getting Started

R is a programming language and software environment for statistical analysis, graphics representation and reporting. R was created by Ross Ihaka and Robert Gentleman at the University of Auckland, New Zealand, and is currently developed by the R Development Core Team. R is freely available under the GNU General Public License, and pre-compiled binary versions are provided for various operating systems like Linux, Windows and Mac. This programming language was named R, based on the first letter of first name of the two R authors (Robert Gentleman and Ross Ihaka), and partly a play on the name of the Bell Labs Language S.

As stated earlier, R is a programming language and software environment for statistical analysis, graphics representation and reporting. The following are the important features of R –

- R is a well-developed, simple and effective programming language which includes conditionals, loops, user defined recursive functions and input and output facilities.
- R has an effective data handling and storage facility,
- R provides a suite of operators for calculations on arrays, lists, vectors and matrices.
- R provides a large, coherent and integrated collection of tools for data analysis.

- R provides graphical facilities for data analysis and display either directly at the computer or printing at the papers.

3.1.1 Environmental Setup

Windows: You can download the Windows installer version of R from R-3.2.2 for Windows (32/64 bit) and save it in a local directory.

As it is a Windows installer (.exe) with a name "R-version-win.exe". You can just double click and run the installer accepting the default settings. If your Windows is 32-bit version, it installs the 32-bit version. But if your windows is 64-bit, then it installs both the 32-bit and 64-bit versions.

After installation you can locate the icon to run the Program in a directory structure "R\R3.2.2\bin\i386\Rgui.exe" under the Windows Program Files. Clicking this icon brings up the R-GUI which is the R console to do R Programming.

Linux: R is available as a binary for many versions of Linux at the location R Binaries.

The instruction to install Linux varies from flavor to flavor. These steps are mentioned under each type of Linux version in the mentioned link. However, if you are in a hurry, then you can use yum command to install R as follows –

```
$ yum install R
```

Above command will install core functionality of R programming along with standard packages, still you need additional package, then you can launch R prompt as follows –

$ R

R version 3.2.0 (2015-04-16) -- "Full of Ingredients"

Copyright (C) 2015 The R Foundation for Statistical Computing

Platform: x86_64-redhat-linux-gnu (64-bit)

R is free software and comes with ABSOLUTELY NO WARRANTY.

You are welcome to redistribute it under certain conditions.

Type 'license()' or 'licence()' for distribution details.

R is a collaborative project with many contributors.

Type 'contributors()' for more information and

'citation()' on how to cite R or R packages in publications.

Type 'demo()' for some demos, 'help()' for on-line help, or

'help.start()' for an HTML browser interface to help.

Type 'q()' to quit R.

\>

3.2 Data Types

Generally, while doing programming in any programming language, you need to use various variables to store various information. Variables are nothing but reserved memory locations to store values. This means that, when you create a variable you reserve some space in memory.

You may like to store information of various data types like character, wide character, integer, floating point, double floating point, Boolean etc. Based on the data type of a variable, the operating system allocates memory and decides what can be stored in the reserved memory.

In contrast to other programming languages like C and java in R, the variables are not declared as some data type. The variables are assigned with R-Objects and the data type of the R-object becomes the data type of the variable. There are many types of R-objects. The frequently used ones are –

- Vectors
- Lists

- Matrices
- Arrays
- Factors
- Data Frames

The simplest of these objects is the **vector object** and there are six data types of these atomic vectors, also termed as six classes of vectors. The other R-Objects are built upon the atomic vectors.

In R programming, the very basic data types are the R-objects called **vectors** which hold elements of different classes as shown above. Please note in R the number of classes is not confined to only the above six types. For example, we can use many atomic vectors and create an array whose class will become array.

Vectors

When you want to create vector with more than one element, you should use **c()** function which means to combine the elements into a vector.

```
# Create a vector.
apple <- c('red','green',"yellow")
print(apple)


# Get the class of the vector.
print(class(apple))
```

Lists

A list is an R-object which can contain many different types of elements inside it like vectors, functions and even another list inside it.

```
# Create a list.

list1 <- list(c(2,5,3),21,3,sin)


# Print the list.

print(list1)
```

Matrices

A matrix is a two-dimensional rectangular data set. It can be created using a vector input to the matrix function.

Arrays

While matrices are confined to two dimensions, arrays can be of any number of dimensions. The array function takes a dim attribute which creates the required number of dimensions. In the below example we create an array with two elements which are 3x3 matrices each.

Factors

Factors are the r-objects which are created using a vector. It stores the vector along with the distinct values of the elements in the vector as labels. The labels are always character irrespective of whether it is numeric or character or Boolean etc. in the input vector. They are useful in statistical modeling.

Factors are created using the **factor()** function. The **nlevels** functions gives the count of levels.

Data Frames

Data frames are tabular data objects. Unlike a matrix in data frame each column can contain different modes of data. The first column can be numeric while the second column can be character and third column can be logical. It is a list of vectors of equal length.

Data Frames are created using the **data.frame()** function.

3.3 Variables

A variable provides us with named storage that our programs can manipulate. A variable in R can store an atomic vector, group of atomic vectors or a combination of many R objects. A valid variable name consists of letters, numbers and the dot or underline characters. The variable name starts with a letter or the dot not followed by a number.

Variable Name	Validity	Reason
var_name2.	valid	Has letters, numbers, dot and underscore
var_name%	Invalid	Has the character '%'. Only dot(.) and underscore allowed.
2var_name	invalid	Starts with a number

.var_name, var.name	valid	Can start with a dot(.) but the dot(.)should not be followed by a number.
.2var_name	invalid	The starting dot is followed by a number making it invalid.
_var_name	invalid	Starts with _ which is not valid

Variable Assignment:

The variables can be assigned values using leftward, rightward and equal to operator. The values of the variables can be printed using **print()** or **cat()**function. The **cat()** function combines multiple items into a continuous print output.

3.4 Operators

An operator is a symbol that tells the compiler to perform specific mathematical or logical manipulations. R language is rich in built-in operators and provides following types of operators.

Types of Operators

We have the following types of operators in R programming –

- Arithmetic Operators
- Relational Operators
- Logical Operators
- Assignment Operators
- Miscellaneous Operators

Arithmetic Operators

Following table shows the arithmetic operators supported by R language. The operators act on each element of the vector.

Operator	Description	Example
+	Adds two vectors	v <- c(2,5.5,6) t <- c(8, 3, 4) print(v+t) it produces the following result – [1] 10.0 8.5 10.0
–	Subtracts second vector from the first	v <- c(2,5.5,6) t <- c(8, 3, 4) print(v-t) it produces the following result – [1] -6.0 2.5 2.0
*	Multiplies both vectors	v <- c(2,5.5,6) t <- c(8, 3, 4) print(v*t) it produces the following result – [1] 16.0 16.5 24.0
/	Divide the first vector with the second	v <- c(2,5.5,6) t <- c(8, 3, 4) print(v/t) When we execute the above code, it produces the following result – [1] 0.250000 1.833333 1.500000

%%	Give the remainder of the first vector with the second	v <- c(2,5.5,6) t <- c(8, 3, 4) print(v%%t) it produces the following result – [1] 2.0 2.5 2.0
%/%	The result of division of first vector with second (quotient)	v <- c(2,5.5,6) t <- c(8, 3, 4) print(v%/%t) it produces the following result – [1] 0 1 1
^	The first vector raised to the exponent of second vector	v <- c(2,5.5,6) t <- c(8, 3, 4) print(v^t) it produces the following result – [1] 256.000 166.375 1296.000

Relational Operators

Following table shows the relational operators supported by R language. Each element of the first vector is compared with the corresponding element of the second vector. The result of comparison is a Boolean value.

Operator	Description	Example
>	Checks if each element of the first vector is greater than the corresponding element of the second vector.	v <- c(2,5.5,6,9) t <- c(8,2.5,14,9) print(v>t) it produces the following result – [1] FALSE TRUE FALSE FALSE
<	Checks if each element of the first vector is less than the corresponding element of the second vector.	v <- c(2,5.5,6,9) t <- c(8,2.5,14,9) print(v < t) it produces the following result – [1] TRUE FALSE TRUE FALSE
==	Checks if each element of the first vector is equal to the corresponding element of the second vector.	v <- c(2,5.5,6,9) t <- c(8,2.5,14,9) print(v == t) it produces the following result – [1] FALSE FALSE FALSE TRUE
<=	Checks if each element of the first vector is less than or equal to the corresponding element of the second vector.	v <- c(2,5.5,6,9) t <- c(8,2.5,14,9) print(v<=t) it produces the following result – [1] TRUE FALSE TRUE TRUE
>=	Checks if each element	v <- c(2,5.5,6,9)

	of the first vector is greater than or equal to the corresponding element of the second vector.	t <- c(8,2.5,14,9) print(v>=t) it produces the following result – [1] FALSE TRUE FALSE TRUE
!=	Checks if each element of the first vector is unequal to the corresponding element of the second vector.	v <- c(2,5.5,6,9) t <- c(8,2.5,14,9) print(v!=t) it produces the following result – [1] TRUE TRUE TRUE FALSE

Logical Operators

Following table shows the logical operators supported by R language. It is applicable only to vectors of type logical, numeric or complex. All numbers greater than 1 are considered as logical value TRUE.

Each element of the first vector is compared with the corresponding element of the second vector. The result of comparison is a Boolean value.

Operator	Description	Example
&	It is called Element-wise Logical AND operator. It combines each element of the first vector with the corresponding element of the second vector and gives a output TRUE if both the elements are TRUE.	v <- c(3,1,TRUE,2+3i) t <- c(4,1,FALSE,2+3i) print(v&t) it produces the following result – [1] TRUE TRUE FALSE TRUE
|	It is called Element-wise Logical OR operator. It combines each element of the first vector with the corresponding element of the second vector and gives a output TRUE if one the elements is TRUE.	v <- c(3,0,TRUE,2+2i) t <- c(4,0,FALSE,2+3i) print(v|t) it produces the following result – [1] TRUE FALSE TRUE TRUE
!	It is called Logical NOT operator. Takes each element of the vector and gives the opposite logical value.	v <- c(3,0,TRUE,2+2i) print(!v) it produces the following result – [1] FALSE TRUE FALSE FALSE

3.5 Decision Making

Decision making structures require the programmer to specify one or more conditions to be evaluated or tested by the program, along with a statement or statements to be executed if the condition is determined to be **true**, and optionally, other statements to be executed if the condition is determined to be **false**.

An **if** statement can be followed by an optional **else** statement which executes when the Boolean expression is false.

```
x <- c("what","is","truth")


if("Truth" %in% x) {

  print("Truth is found")

} else {

  print("Truth is not found")

}
```

When the above code is compiled and executed, it produces the following result –

```
[1] "Truth is not found"
```

An **if** statement can be followed by an optional **else if...else** statement, which is very useful to test various conditions using single if...else if statement.

When using **if**, **else if**, **else** statements there are few points to keep in mind.

- An **if** can have zero or one **else** and it must come after any **else if**'s.

- An **if** can have zero to many **else if's** and they must come before the else.

- Once an **else if** succeeds, none of the remaining **else if**'s or **else**'s will be tested.

3.6 Loops

There may be a situation when you need to execute a block of code several number of times. In general, statements are executed sequentially. The first statement in a function is executed first, followed by the second, and so on.

Programming languages provide various control structures that allow for more complicated execution paths.

While Loop:

The While loop executes the same code again and again until a stop condition is met.

```
v <- c("Hello","while loop")
```

```
cnt <- 2


while (cnt < 7) {

  print(v)

  cnt = cnt + 1

}
```

When the above code is compiled and executed, it produces the following result –

```
[1] "Hello"  "while loop"
[1] "Hello"  "while loop"
[1] "Hello"  "while loop"
[1] "Hello"  "while loop"
[1] "Hello"  "while loop"
```

For Loop:

A **For loop** is a repetition control structure that allows you to efficiently write a loop that needs to execute a specific number of times.

```
v <- LETTERS[1:4]

for ( i in v) {

  print(i)

}
```

When the above code is compiled and executed, it produces the following result –

```
[1] "A"
[1] "B"
[1] "C"
[1] "D"
```

3.7 Functions

A function is a set of statements organized together to perform a specific task. R has a large number of in-built functions and the user can create their own functions.

In R, a function is an object so the R interpreter is able to pass control to the function, along with arguments that may be necessary for the function to accomplish the actions.

The function in turn performs its task and returns control to the interpreter as well as any result which may be stored in other objects.

Function Components

The different parts of a function are –

- Function Name – This is the actual name of the function. It is stored in R environment as an object with this name.
- Arguments – An argument is a placeholder. When a function is invoked, you pass a value to the argument. Arguments are optional; that is, a

function may contain no arguments. Also, arguments can have default values.
- Function Body – The function body contains a collection of statements that defines what the function does.
- Return Value – The return value of a function is the last expression in the function body to be evaluated.

R has many in-built functions which can be directly called in the program without defining them first. We can also create and use our own functions referred as user defined functions.

```
# Create a function to print squares of numbers in sequence.

new.function <- function(a) {

  for(i in 1:a) {

    b <- i^2

    print(b)

  }

}
```

R packages are a collection of R functions, complied code and sample data. They are stored under a directory called "library" in the R environment. By default, R installs a set of packages during installation. More packages are added later, when they are needed for some specific purpose. When we start the R console, only the default packages are available by default. Other packages which are already installed have to be loaded explicitly to be used by the R program that is going to use them.

Chapter 4

Types of Machine Learning

Learning means the acquisition of knowledge or skills through study or experience. Based on this, we can define machine learning (ML) as follows –

It may be defined as the field of computer science, more specifically an application of artificial intelligence, which provides computer systems the ability to learn with data and improve from experience without being explicitly programmed.

Basically, the main focus of machine learning is to allow the computers learn automatically without human intervention. Now the question arises that how such learning can be started and done? It can be started with the observations of data. The data can be some examples, instruction or some direct experiences too. Then on the basis of this input, machine makes better decision by looking for some patterns in data.

4.1 Types of Machine Learning

Machine Learning Algorithms helps computer system learn without being explicitly programmed. These algorithms are categorized into supervised or unsupervised.

- Supervised Machine Learning
- Unsupervised Machine Learning
- Reinforcement Machine Learning

4.1.1 Supervised Machine Learning

This is the most commonly used machine learning algorithm. It is called supervised because the process of algorithm learning from the training dataset can be thought of as a teacher supervising the learning process. In this kind of ML algorithm, the possible outcomes are already known and training data is also labeled with correct answers. It can be understood as follows –

Suppose we have input variables **x** and an output variable **y** and we applied an algorithm to learn the mapping function from the input to output such as –

$$Y = f(x)$$

Now, the main goal is to approximate the mapping function so well that when we have new input data (x), we can predict the output variable (Y) for that data.

Mainly supervised leaning problems can be divided into the following two kinds of problems –

- **Classification** – A problem is called classification problem when we have the categorized output such as "black", "teaching", "non-teaching", etc.

- **Regression** – A problem is called regression problem when we have the real value output such as "distance", "kilogram", etc.

Decision tree, random forest, KNN, logistic regression are the examples of supervised machine learning algorithms.

4.1.2 Unsupervised Machine Learning

As the name suggests, these kinds of machine learning algorithms do not have any supervisor to provide any sort of guidance. That is why unsupervised machine learning algorithms are closely aligned with what some call true artificial intelligence. It can be understood as follows –

Suppose we have input variable x, then there will be no corresponding output variables as there is in supervised learning algorithms.

In simple words, we can say that in unsupervised learning there will be no correct answer and no teacher for the guidance. Algorithms help to discover interesting patterns in data.

Unsupervised learning problems can be divided into the following two kinds of problem –

- **Clustering** – In clustering problems, we need to discover the inherent groupings in the data. For example, grouping customers by their purchasing behavior.

- **Association** – A problem is called association problem because such kinds of problem require discovering the rules that describe large portions of our data. For example, finding the customers who buy both **x** and **y**.

K-means for clustering, Apriori algorithm for association are the examples of unsupervised machine learning algorithms.

4.1.3 Reinforcement Machine Learning

These kinds of machine learning algorithms are used very less. These algorithms train the systems to make specific decisions. Basically, the machine is exposed to an environment where it trains itself continually using the trial and error method. These algorithms learn from past experience and tries to capture the best possible knowledge to make accurate decisions. Markov Decision Process is an example of reinforcement machine learning algorithms.

4.2 Data Processing

We have already studied supervised as well as unsupervised machine learning algorithms. These algorithms require formatted data to start the training process. We must prepare or format data in a certain way so that it can be supplied as an input to ML algorithms.

This section focuses on data preparation for machine learning algorithms.

In our daily life, we deal with lots of data but this data is in raw form. To provide the data as the input of machine learning algorithms, we need to convert it into a meaningful data. That is where data preprocessing comes into picture. In other simple words, we can say that before providing the data to the machine learning algorithms we need to preprocess the data.

Steps:

Follow these steps to preprocess the data in Python –

Step 1 – Importing the useful packages – If we are using Python then this would be the first step for converting the data into a certain format, i.e., preprocessing. It can be done as follows –

```
import numpy as np
sklearn import preprocessing
```

Here we have used the following two packages –

- **NumPy** – Basically NumPy is a general purpose array-processing package designed to efficiently manipulate large multi-dimensional arrays of arbitrary records without sacrificing too much speed for small multi-dimensional arrays.

- **Sklearn.preprocessing** – This package provides many common utility functions and transformer classes to change raw feature vectors into a representation that is more suitable for machine learning algorithms.

Step 2 – Defining sample data – After importing the packages, we need to define some sample data so that we can apply preprocessing techniques on that data. We will now define the following sample data –

```
Input_data = np.array([2.1, -1.9, 5.5],

        [-1.5, 2.4, 3.5],

        [0.5, -7.9, 5.6],

        [5.9, 2.3, -5.8]])
```

Step3 – Applying preprocessing technique – In this step, we need to apply any of the preprocessing techniques.

The following section describes the data preprocessing techniques.

4.2.1 Techniques for Data Preprocessing

The techniques for data preprocessing are described below –

Binarization

This is the preprocessing technique which is used when we need to convert our numerical values into Boolean values. We can use an inbuilt method to binarize the input data say by using 0.5 as the threshold value in the following way –

```
data_binarized = preprocessing.Binarizer(threshold
= 0.5).transform(input_data)

print("\nBinarized data:\n", data_binarized)
```

Now, after running the above code we will get the following output, all the values above 0.5(threshold value) would be converted to 1 and all the values below 0.5 would be converted to 0.

Binarized data

```
[[ 1. 0. 1.]
 [ 0. 1. 1.]
 [ 0. 0. 1.]
 [ 1. 1. 0.]]
```

Mean Removal

It is another very common preprocessing technique that is used in machine learning. Basically it is used to eliminate the mean from feature vector so that every feature is centered on zero. We can also remove the bias from the features in the feature vector. For applying mean removal preprocessing technique on the sample data, we can write the Python code shown below. The code will display the Mean and Standard deviation of the input data −

```
print("Mean = ", input_data.mean(axis = 0))
print("Std deviation = ", input_data.std(axis = 0))
```

We will get the following output after running the above lines of code –

```
    Mean = [ 1.75    -1.275    2.2]
Std deviation = [ 2.71431391  4.20022321
4.69414529]
```

Now, the code below will remove the Mean and Standard deviation of the input data –

```
data_scaled = preprocessing.scale(input_data)

print("Mean =", data_scaled.mean(axis=0))

print("Std deviation =", data_scaled.std(axis = 0))
```

We will get the following output after running the above lines of code –

```
    Mean = [ 1.11022302e-16 0.00000000e+00
0.00000000e+00]
Std deviation = [ 1.       1.       1.]
```

Scaling

It is another data preprocessing technique that is used to scale the feature vectors. Scaling of feature vectors is needed because the values of every feature can vary between many random values. In other words, we can say that scaling is important because we do not want any feature to be synthetically large or small. With the help of the following Python code, we can do the scaling of our input data, i.e., feature vector –

Min max scaling

```
data_scaler_minmax = preprocessing.MinMaxScaler(feature_range=(0,1))

data_scaled_minmax = data_scaler_minmax.fit_transform(input_data)

print ("\nMin max scaled data:\n", data_scaled_minmax)
```

We will get the following output after running the above lines of code –

Min max scaled data

```
[[ 0.48648649  0.58252427  0.99122807]
 [ 0.          1.          0.81578947]
 [ 0.27027027  0.          1.        ]
 [ 1.          0.99029126  0.        ]]
```

Chapter 5
Regression & Classification

5.1 Regression

Regression techniques are one of the most popular statistical techniques used for predictive modeling and data mining tasks. On average, analytics professionals know only 2-3 types of regression which are commonly used in real world. They are linear and logistic regression. But the fact is there are more than 10 types of regression algorithms designed for various types of analysis. Each type has its own significance. Every analyst must know which form of regression to use depending on type of data and distribution.

5.1.1 Regression Analysis

Let's take a simple example: Suppose your manager asked you to predict annual sales. There can be a hundred of factors (drivers) that affects sales. In this case, sales are your dependent variable. Factors affecting sales are independent variables. Regression analysis would help you to solve this problem.

In simple words, regression analysis is used to model the relationship between a dependent variable and one or more independent variables.

It helps us to answer the following questions –

1. Which of the drivers have a significant impact on sales?
2. Which is the most important driver of sales

3. How do the drivers interact with each other?
4. What would be the annual sales next year.

5.1.2 Terminologies

- **Outliers:**
  Suppose there is an observation in the dataset which is having a very high or very low value as compared to the other observations in the data, i.e. it does not belong to the population, such an observation is called an outlier. In simple words, it is extreme value. An outlier is a problem because many times it hampers the results we get.

- **Multicollinearity:**
  When the independent variables are highly correlated to each other than the variables are said to be multicollinear. Many types of regression techniques assume multicollinearity should not be present in the dataset. It is because it causes problems in ranking variables based on its importance. Or it makes job difficult in selecting the most important independent variable (factor).

- **Heteroscedasticity:**
  When dependent variable's variability is not equal across values of an independent variable, it is called heteroscedasticity.

Example – As one's income increases, the variability of food consumption will increase. A poorer person will spend a rather constant amount by always eating inexpensive food; a wealthier person may occasionally buy inexpensive food and at other times eat expensive meals. Those with higher incomes display a greater variability of food consumption.

- **Underfitting & Overfitting:**

  When we use unnecessary explanatory variables, it might lead to overfitting. Overfitting means that our algorithm works well on the training set but is unable to perform better on the test sets. It is also known as problem of high variance.

  When our algorithm works so poorly that it is unable to fit even training set well then it is said to underfit the data. It is also known as problem of high bias.

5.1.3 Types of Regression

Every regression technique has some assumptions attached to it which we need to meet before running analysis. These techniques differ in terms of type of dependent and independent variables and distribution.

5.1.3.1 Linear Aggression

It is one of the most well-known algorithms in statistics and machine learning.

Basic concept − Mainly linear regression is a linear model that assumes a linear relationship between the input variables say x and the single output variable say y. In other words, we can say that y can be calculated from a linear combination of the input variables x. The relationship between variables can be established by fitting a best line.

Types of Linear Regression

Linear regression is of the following two types −

Simple linear regression − A linear regression algorithm is called simple linear regression if it is having only one independent variable.

Multiple linear regression − A linear regression algorithm is called multiple linear regression if it is having more than one independent variable.

Linear regression is mainly used to estimate the real values based on continuous variable(s). For example, the total sale of a shop in a day, based on real values, can be estimated by linear regression.

5.1.3.2 Polynomial Regression

Polynomial regression is a form of regression analysis in which the relationship between the independent variable x and the dependent variable y is modelled as an nth degree polynomial in x. Polynomial regression fits a nonlinear relationship between the value of x and the corresponding conditional mean of y, denoted $E(y \mid x)$,

5.1.3.3 Quantile Regression

Quantile regression is the extension of linear regression and we generally use it when outliers, high skewedness and heteroscedasticity exist in the data.

In linear regression, we predict the mean of the dependent variable for given independent variables. Since mean does not describe the whole distribution, so modeling the mean is not a full description of a relationship between dependent and independent variables. So, we can use quantile regression which predicts a quantile (or percentile) for given independent variables.

5.1.3.4 Lasso Regression

Lasso stands for Least Absolute Shrinkage and Selection Operator. It makes use of L1 regularization technique in the objective function.

5.1.3.5 Elastic Net Regression

Elastic Net regression is preferred over both ridge and lasso regression when one is dealing with highly correlated independent variables.

5.1.3.6 Principal Components Regression

PCR is a regression technique which is widely used when you have many independent variables OR multicollinearity exist in your data.

5.1.3.7 Support Vector Regression

Support vector regression can solve both linear and non-linear models. SVM uses non-linear kernel functions (such as polynomial) to find the optimal solution for non-linear models. The main idea of SVR is to minimize error, individualizing the hyperplane which maximizes the margin.

5.1.3.8 Ordinal Regression

Ordinal Regression is used to predict ranked values. In simple words, this type of regression is suitable when dependent variable is ordinal in nature.

5.2 Classification

In machine learning and statistics, classification is a supervised learning approach in which the computer program learns from the data input given to it and then uses this learning to classify new observation. This data set may simply be bi-class (like identifying whether the person is male or female or that the mail is spam or non-spam) or it may be multi-class too. Some examples of classification problems are: speech recognition, handwriting recognition, bio metric identification, document classification etc.

5.2.1 Terminologies

Classification can be performed on structured or unstructured data. Classification is a technique where we categorize data into a given number of classes. The main goal of a classification problem is to identify the category/class to which a new data will fall under.

Few of the terminologies encountered in machine learning – classification:

- **Classifier:** An algorithm that maps the input data to a specific category.

- **Classification model:** A classification model tries to draw some conclusion from the input values given for training. It will predict the class labels/categories for the new data.

- **Feature:** A feature is an individual measurable property of a phenomenon being observed.

- **Binary Classification:** Classification task with two possible outcomes. Eg: Gender classification (Male / Female)

- **Multi class classification:** Classification with more than two classes. In multi class classification each sample is assigned to one and only one target label. Eg: An animal can be cat or dog but not both at the same time

- **Multi label classification:** Classification task where each sample is mapped to a set of target labels (more than one class). Eg: A news article can be about sports, a person, and location at the same time.

The following are the steps involved in building a classification model:

- **Initialize** the classifier to be used.

- **Train the classifier:** All classifiers in scikit-learn uses a fit(X, y) method to fit the model(training) for the given train data X and train label y.

- **Predict the target:** Given an unlabeled observation X, the predict(X) returns the predicted label y.

- **Evaluate** the classifier model

5.2.2 Types of Classification

Here we have the types of classification algorithms in Machine Learning:

5.2.2.1 Logistics Regression

It is a classification algorithm and also known as logit regression. It is a statistical method for analyzing a data set in which there are one or more independent variables that determine an outcome. The outcome is measured with a dichotomous variable (in which there are only two possible outcomes). The goal of logistic regression is to find the best fitting model to describe the relationship between the dichotomous characteristic of interest (dependent variable = response or outcome variable) and a set of independent (predictor or explanatory) variables.

5.2.2.2 Naïve Bayes

It is also a classification technique. The logic behind this classification technique is to use Bayes theorem for building classifiers. The assumption is that the predictors are independent. In simple words, it assumes that the presence of a particular feature in a class is unrelated to the presence of any other feature. Below is the equation for Bayes theorem

$$P\left(\frac{A}{B}\right) = \frac{P\left(\frac{B}{A}\right)P(A)}{P(B)}$$

The Naïve Bayes model is easy to build and particularly useful for large data sets.

5.2.2.3 Decision Tree

Decision tree is a supervised learning algorithm that is mostly used for classification problems. Basically, it is a classifier expressed as recursive partition based on the independent variables. Decision tree has nodes which form the rooted tree. Rooted tree is a directed tree with a node called "root". Root does not have any incoming edges and all the other nodes have one incoming edge. These nodes are called leaves or decision nodes. For example, consider the following decision tree to see whether a person is fit or not.

5.2.2.4 Random Forest

It is a supervised classification algorithm. The advantage of random forest algorithm is that it can be used for both classification and regression kind of problems. Basically, it is the collection of decision trees (i.e., forest) or you can say ensemble of the decision trees. The basic concept of random forest is that each tree gives a classification and the forest chooses the best classifications from them. Followings are the advantages of Random Forest algorithm –

- Random forest classifier can be used for both classification and regression tasks.
- They can handle the missing values.
- It won't over fit the model even if we have a greater number of trees in the forest.

5.2.2.5 K Nearest Neighbor (KNN)

It is used for both classification and regression of the problems. It is widely used to solve classification problems. The main concept of this algorithm is that it used to store all the available cases and classifies new cases by majority votes of its k neighbors. The case being then assigned to the class which is the most common amongst its K-nearest neighbors, measured by a distance function. The distance function can be Euclidean, Minkowski and Hamming distance. Consider the following to use KNN –

- Computationally KNN are expensive than other algorithms used for classification problems.
- The normalization of variables needed otherwise higher range variables can bias it.
- In KNN, we need to work on pre-processing stage like noise removal.

5.2.2.6 Support Vector Machine

It is used for both classification and regression problems. But mainly it is used for classification problems. The main concept of SVM is to plot each data item as a point in n-dimensional space with the value of each feature being the value of a particular coordinate. Here n would be the features we would have.

Chapter 6

Clustering

Unsupervised machine learning algorithms do not have any supervisor to provide any sort of guidance. That is why they are closely aligned with what some call true artificial intelligence.

In unsupervised learning, there would be no correct answer and no teacher for the guidance. Algorithms need to discover the interesting pattern in data for learning.

6.1 Introduction

Basically, it is a type of unsupervised learning method and a common technique for statistical data analysis used in many fields. Clustering mainly is a task of dividing the set of observations into subsets, called clusters, in such a way that observations in the same cluster are similar in one sense and they are dissimilar to the observations in other clusters. In simple words, we can say that the main goal of clustering is to group the data on the basis of similarity and dissimilarity.

Clustering is the task of dividing the population or data points into a number of groups such that data points in the same groups are more similar to other data points in the same group and dissimilar to the data points in other groups. It is basically a collection of objects on the basis of similarity and dissimilarity between them.

Clustering is very much important as it determines the intrinsic grouping among the unlabeled data present. There are no criteria for a good clustering. It depends on the user, what is the criteria they may use which satisfy their need. For instance, we could be interested in finding representatives for homogeneous groups (data reduction), in finding "natural clusters" and describe their unknown properties ("natural" data types), in finding useful and suitable groupings ("useful" data classes) or in finding unusual data objects (outlier detection). This algorithm must make some assumptions which constitute the similarity of points and each assumption make different and equally valid clusters.

6.2 Types of Clustering Methods

Following are types of Clustering methods.

6.2.1 Distribution Based Method

It is a clustering model in which we will fit the data on the probability that how it may belong to the same distribution. The grouping done may be normal or gaussian. Gaussian distribution is more prominent where we have fixed number of distributions and all the upcoming data is fitted into it such that the distribution of data may get maximize. This model works good on synthetic data and diversely sized clusters. But this model may have problem if the constraints are not used to limit model's complexity. Furthermore, Distribution-based clustering produces clusters which assume concisely defined mathematical models underlying the data, a rather strong assumption for some data distributions. For Ex- Expectation-maximization algorithm which uses multivariate normal distributions is one of popular example of this algorithm.

6.2.2 Centroid Based Method

This is basically one of iterative clustering algorithm in which the clusters are formed by the closeness of data points to the centroid of clusters. Here, the cluster center i.e. centroid is formed such that the distance of data points is minimum with the center. This problem is basically one of NP- Hard problem and thus solutions are commonly approximated over a number of trails.

6.2.3 Connectivity Based Methods

The core idea of connectivity based model is similar to Centroid based model which is basically defining clusters on the basis of closeness of data points .Here we work on a notion that the data points which are closer have similar behavior as compared to data points that are farther. It is not a single partitioning of the data set , instead it provides an extensive hierarchy of clusters that merge with each other at certain distances. Here the choice of distance function is subjective. These models are very easy to interpret but it lacks scalability.

6.2.4 Density Models

In this clustering model there will be a searching of data space for areas of varied density of data points in the data space. It isolates various density regions based on different densities present in the data space.

6.3 Clustering Algorithms

The clustering Algorithms are of many types. The following overview will only list the most prominent examples of clustering algorithms, as there are possibly over 100 published clustering algorithms. Not all provide models for their clusters and can thus not easily be categorized.

6.3.1 K-Means Clustering

It is the simplest unsupervised learning algorithm that solves clustering problem. K-means algorithm partition n observations into k clusters where each observation belongs to the cluster with the nearest mean serving as a prototype of the cluster.

The algorithm works as follows:

- First, we initialize k points, called means, randomly.
- We categorize each item to its closest mean and we update the mean's coordinates, which are the averages of the items categorized in that mean so far.
- We repeat the process for a given number of iterations and at the end, we have our clusters.

6.4 Applications

Applications of Clustering in different fields

- **Marketing:** It can be used to characterize & discover customer segments for marketing purposes.
- **Biology:** It can be used for classification among different species of plants and animals.
- **Libraries:** It is used in clustering different books on the basis of topics and information.

- **Insurance:** It is used to acknowledge the customers, their policies and identifying the frauds.
- **City Planning:** It is used to make groups of houses and to study their values based on their geographical locations and other factors present.
- **Earthquake studies:** By learning the earthquake affected areas we can determine the dangerous zones.

Chapter 7

Natural Language Processing, Reinforcement Learning

7.1 Natural Language Processing

Humans have been writing things down for thousands of years. Over that time, our brain has gained a tremendous amount of experience in understanding natural language. When we read something written on a piece of paper or in a blog post on the internet, we understand what that thing really means in the real-world. We feel the emotions that reading that thing elicits and we often visualize how that thing would look in real life.

Natural Language Processing (NLP) is a sub-field of Artificial Intelligence that is focused on enabling computers to understand and process human languages, to get computers closer to a human-level understanding of language. Computers don't yet have the same intuitive understanding of natural language that humans do. They can't really understand what the language is really trying to say. In a nutshell, a computer can't read between the lines.

NLP is a way for computers to analyze, understand, and derive meaning from human language in a smart and useful way. By utilizing NLP, developers can organize and structure knowledge to perform tasks such as automatic summarization, translation, named entity recognition, relationship extraction, sentiment analysis, speech recognition, and topic segmentation.

That being said, recent advances in Machine Learning (ML) have enabled computers to do quite a lot of useful things with natural language! Deep Learning has enabled us to write programs to perform things like language translation, semantic understanding, and text summarization. All of these things add real-world value, making it easy for you to understand and perform computations on large blocks of text without the manual effort.

The development of NLP has its meaning because of some specific problems and phenomena that arrive when we study natural language. Most of the times, these problems are unique in comparison to the problems that emerge in other fields of computer science or engineering, and that is in part what makes NLP such an interesting and different area.

7.1.1 Introduction

Natural Language Processing (NLP) refers to AI method of communicating with intelligent systems using a natural language such as English.

Processing of Natural Language is required when you want an intelligent system like robot to perform as per your instructions, when you want to hear decision from a dialogue based clinical expert system, etc.

The field of NLP involves making computers reform useful tasks with the natural languages humans use. The input and output of an NLP system can be –

- Speech

- Written Text

7.1.2 Components of NLP

In this section, we will learn about the different components of NLP. There are two components of NLP. The components are described below –

Natural Language Understanding (NLU)

It involves the following tasks –

- Mapping the given input in natural language into useful representations.
- Analyzing different aspects of the language.

Natural Language Generation (NLG)

It is the process of producing meaningful phrases and sentences in the form of natural language from some internal representation. It involves –

- Text planning – This includes retrieving the relevant content from the knowledge base.
- Sentence planning – This includes choosing the required words, forming meaningful phrases, setting tone of the sentence.
- Text Realization – This is mapping sentence plan into sentence structure.

7.1.3 NLP Terminology

Let us now see a few important terms in the NLP terminology.

Phonology – It is study of organizing sound systematically.

Morphology – It is a study of construction of words from primitive meaningful units.

Morpheme – It is a primitive unit of meaning in a language.

Syntax – It refers to arranging words to make a sentence. It also involves determining the structural role of words in the sentence and in phrases.

Semantics – It is concerned with the meaning of words and how to combine words into meaningful phrases and sentences.

Pragmatics – It deals with using and understanding sentences in different situations and how the interpretation of the sentence is affected.

Discourse – It deals with how the immediately preceding sentence can affect the interpretation of the next sentence.

World Knowledge – It includes the general knowledge about the world.

7.2 Reinforcement Learning

This type of learning is used to reinforce or strengthen the network based on critic information. That is, a network being trained under reinforcement learning, receives some feedback from the environment. However, the feedback is evaluative and not instructive as in the case of supervised learning. Based on this feedback, the network performs the adjustments of the weights to obtain better critic information in future.

Reinforcement learning is an approach to machine learning that is inspired by behaviorist psychology. It is similar to how a child learns to perform a new task. Reinforcement learning contrasts with other machine learning approaches in that the algorithm is not explicitly told how to perform a task, but works through the problem on its own.

As an agent, which could be a self-driving car or a program playing chess, interacts with its environment, receives a reward state depending on how it performs, such as driving to destination safely or winning a game. Conversely, the agent receives a penalty for performing incorrectly, such as going off the road or being checkmated.

The agent over time makes decisions to maximize its reward and minimize its penalty using dynamic programming. The advantage of this approach to artificial intelligence is that it allows an AI program to learn without a programmer spelling out how an agent should perform the task.

This learning process is similar to supervised learning but we might have very less information.

7.2.1 Building Blocks: Environment and Agent

Environment and Agent are main building blocks of reinforcement learning in AI. This section discusses them in detail –

Agent:

- An agent is anything that can perceive its environment through sensors and acts upon that environment through effectors.
- A human agent has sensory organs such as eyes, ears, nose, tongue and skin parallel to the sensors, and other organs such as hands, legs, mouth, for effectors.
- A robotic agent replaces cameras and infrared range finders for the sensors, and various motors and actuators for effectors.
- A software agent has encoded bit strings as its programs and actions.

Agent Terminology:

The following terms are more frequently used in reinforcement learning in AI –

- Performance Measure of Agent – It is the criteria, which determines how successful an agent is.
- Behavior of Agent – It is the action that agent performs after any given sequence of percepts.
- Percept – It is agent's perceptual inputs at a given instance.
- Percept Sequence – It is the history of all that an agent has perceived till date.
- Agent Function – It is a map from the precept sequence to an action.

Environment:

Some programs operate in an entirely artificial environment confined to keyboard input, database, computer file systems and character output on a screen.

In contrast, some software agents, such as software robots or softbots, exist in rich and unlimited softbot domains. The simulator has a very detailed, and complex environment. The software agent needs to choose from a long array of actions in real time.

For example, a softbot designed to scan the online preferences of the customer and display interesting items to the customer works in the real as well as an artificial environment.

Chapter 8
Conclusion

8.1 Conclusion

Machine learning is a subfield of artificial intelligence (AI). The goal of machine learning generally is to understand the structure of data and fit that data into models that can be understood and utilized by people.

Although machine learning is a field within computer science, it differs from traditional computational approaches. In traditional computing, algorithms are sets of explicitly programmed instructions used by computers to calculate or problem solve. Machine learning algorithms instead allow for computers to train on data inputs and use statistical analysis in order to output values that fall within a specific range. Because of this, machine learning facilitates computers in building models from sample data in order to automate decision-making processes based on data inputs.

Any technology user today has benefitted from machine learning. Facial recognition technology allows social media platforms to help users tag and share photos of friends. Optical character recognition (OCR) technology converts images of text into movable type. Recommendation engines, powered by machine learning, suggest what movies or television shows to watch next based on user preferences. Self-driving cars that rely on machine learning to navigate may soon be available to consumers.

We hope you have enjoyed learning about "Intermediate's Guide for Machine Learning with R/Python". Machine learning is a continuously developing field. Because of this, there are some considerations to keep in mind as you work with machine learning methodologies, or analyze the impact of machine learning processes. Machine learning is a continuously developing field. Because of this, there are some considerations to keep in mind as you work with machine learning methodologies, or analyze the impact of machine learning processes.

Two of the most widely adopted machine learning methods are supervised learning which trains algorithms based on example input and output data that is labeled by humans, and unsupervised learning which provides the algorithm with no labeled data in order to allow it to find structure within its input data.

www.ingramcontent.com/pod-product-compliance
Lightning Source LLC
Chambersburg PA
CBHW020453220526
45464CB00002B/978